CARRIERS:

The Emergence of True Worshippers

CARRIERS:

The Emergence of True Worshippers

Ish Chayil & Eshet Chayil

CRYSTAL L. PLEASANT

XULON PRESS

Xulon Press
2301 Lucien Way #415
Maitland, FL 32751
407.339.4217
www.xulonpress.com

Paperback ISBN-13: 978-1-66283-157-7

DEDICATION

To Kingdom Daughters of KDR, who have heard and answered the Higher Call and are convinced that you exist to serve our King in the global advancement of His Kingdom Agenda! As a result, each of you have deliberately cultivated your Kingdom Orientation and embraced your Kingdom Identity! You now experience your journey anew, as you align with the Father's will, hearing His voice and following His lead. The presence of the King has become Your reality and His will your motivation! May you continue to manifest His presence wherever you are stationed, and *make things better*! We have gathered over the past 5 years to this end… What an honor it is to serve you all!

To men and women who are discovering that there's more to your existence than what meets the eye! May these writings serve as divine tools to facilitate clarity of purpose, and a fresh revelation of the King's desire to be apart of your every day existence. May you realize His marvelous will, which involves your recruitment into His great global Let There Be Light Campaign! May you see life anew as His Word illuminates your heart and your path! May the sound of His voice become ever so clear, and your desire to follow His lead intensifies as you encounter Him!

To my husband and children: You are expressions of God's love and faithfulness to me! As a family, may we live out His will and purpose, and represent Him well! May the King's desire and Cause forever be ours!

To my King! May Your glory cover the earth, as the waters cover the sea! May Your great Light cancel darkness in all its forms! May your sons and daughters live as extensions of Your powerful work through the Son, Jesus Christ! May we magnify You by allowing Your explosive *chayil* attributes to be expressed through us! May we bear witness of the presence of Your Kingdom!

I have abandoned myself to Your purposes! Its in You that I find my existence and identity! I honor You with every breath I breathe!

FOREWORD

God always has a definite man or woman, to accomplish a definite task at a definite time, for results that will affect so many. This is such an incredible timely writing for the body of Christ and for the world. I place this collection in the category of the word found in the explanation writings of Proverbs.

"A word fitly spoken is like apples of gold in pictures of silver" (Proverbs 25:11).

Thank you Crystal for hearing and obeying, for the purpose of our knowing and understanding who we are as Carriers of His presence as True Worshippers.

Bishop George Searight
Abundant Life Family Worship Church
New Brunswick, NJ

CONTENTS

PREFACE

This third volume of my Chayil Collection takes its title from John chapter 4, though its inspiration originates from a passage in the previous volume. The message contains a Holy Spirit cry for spiritual insight, sensitivity, and discernment of seasons, which I strongly believe was the same cry for 2020, the year of the "Great Pandemic," but most importantly, the year of clarity of vision and purpose to facilitate personal alignment with the King's desire and demand! Coincidentally, the cry above also parallels that of 2 Chronicles 7:14, possibly one of the most popular passages preached throughout the quarantine: repent, refocus, reset, and anticipate revival!

The narrative opens with Jesus announcing that He must defy conventional and societal restrictions by going to a place where those who were considered outsiders lived, something that would only further disrupt Jesus's connecting with the religious establishment of His day. Both groups read the same Scripture and worshipped the same God, but they expressed their faith differently. Does this sound familiar? Historically, the Jews would go out of their way to avoid Samaritans, the total opposite of what Jesus was doing in verse 4, "But He needed to go through Samaria" (NKJV).

In a time when the number of likes and followers is the common motivating factor in the world, Jesus was on a mission to minister to the life of **one** person, a female, who lived in the wrong place and was born to the wrong people. Not only was her gender and ethnicity a problem, so were her social status, lifestyle, and even her town. Yet, God had a plan, purpose, and assignment for this lady, and she was important enough for Him to send His only begotten Son to spend time with her.

Jesus's request of this woman was a divine setup: "Give Me a drink" (4:7). He was there to break traditional barriers and completely transform this woman's life! The dialogue that followed was one where spiritual insight was a problem, as she was completely unaware of Jesus's identity and unable to recognize the authentic presence of the Messiah. Sensitivity was also a problem, as she struggled to see pass their differences and misinterpreted what Jesus was really offering. Discernment of seasons was a huge problem as Jesus explained what was appropriate for the current God-season and the divine shift that it would bring. Speaking of seasons, Jesus foretold of a time when kingdom demands would render traditional religious conventions void and invalid, a time when styles and places of worship would not matter. In this new season, the emphasis would be on the heart of worship. Why? Because the true meaning of Christian worship is a lifestyle of surrender, a consistent act of submission to the Lord. It is to give oneself over to the Lord as His slave or servant. Hence, the state of one's heart directly impacts one's service or worship. A lifestyle of sweet surrender and service to the King is true worship.

Having been transformed by an encounter with Jesus, the Samaritan woman was ignited by His power and became an effective witness, advancing God's Kingdom Agenda! In typical *chayil* agent fashion, she in turn invited others to encounter Him as well! I believe Jesus's dialogue with the Samaritan woman at the well prophetically speaks to the global Body of Christ and serves as a call for activation and alignment, resulting in a powerful, worldwide revival and our Father receiving Great Glory! Jesus further described God's desire for and His active pursuit of True Worshippers, those whose hearts motivate a life of service to Him. Having been in His presence during the quarantine—I mean, "Great Shut-In"—there are those who hear the call to arise in a new state of surrender. Just as the woman at the well was offered living water, or the Water of Life, so the Holy Spirit has poured out of His Spirit on every Kingdom son and daughter, His *chayil* agents. Each *ish chayil* and *eshet chayil* is numbered amongst ignited **Carriers**, manifesting in a powerful **Emergence of True Worshippers** who usher in a fiery revival as they carry the presence of the King to the ends of the earth! Volume III of this Chayil Collection is about them! It's about you and me!

INTRODUCTION

A t the time of this writing, America is struggling to distribute the newly-formulated COVID-19 vaccine to its citizens as we approach nearly 500,000 COVID-related deaths. Many of its cities remain under some form of quarantine, where the normal flow of activities is either greatly restricted, partially limited, or completely forbidden. Indeed, it has been a year that has brought with it much pain, suffering, sorrow, and loss on many levels. Even now, many of us find ourselves in some stage of grief as others are in varying phases of recovery, all while another promised round of stimulus checks hangs in the balances. Additionally, and just as devastating, is the pervasive financial devastation as companies struggle to stay afloat or even open, making feeble attempts to hire new staff as many grasp at every effort to maintain their current housing status and pay their bills. Nations around the globe report the same state of affairs as the world stands in need of miracles! Yet, a divine juxtaposition to this massive global desolation is a great global revival that is causing individuals to return to their first love, the God of their youth, and strengthen their faith and commitment to Him! Indeed, there have been major changes on many levels, resulting in epic worldwide paradigm shifts! I believe these shifts originate in the foundations of the earth and even heaven itself.

2020 will be forever known as the year of the Great COVID-19 Pandemic; however, it will also be remembered as the year of Great Clarity of Vision, Purpose, and Understanding where the Kingdom of God is concerned. I wholeheartedly believe that the world, particularly the global Body of Christ, heard the cry of the Holy Spirit as a higher call was uttered. While I do not believe that YHWH was the source or cause of the pandemic, the Scriptures bear witness of an All-Powerful God who alone has the power to turn what the devil meant for evil into good (Genesis 50:20-21). The Almighty God has a reputation of bringing something beautiful out of that which was utterly horrific: "Can any good thing come out of Nazareth?" (John 1:46) During 2020, I, like many who believe that the God of purpose has loaded every life-season with the same, turned my eyes to 2 Chronicles 7:14 as I sought to understand His will in such turbulent times. Daily I asked, "Father, where are You in this?" I, too, began to sense the Holy Spirit's call to **repent**, meaning to turn or change; to **refocus**, fixing our eyes on Jesus; and to **reset,** defying the pulls of the urgencies of life and other distractions, while we anticipate the great **revival** that our God and King would Himself usher in! As the year ended, I resolved to firmly hold to these lessons as I believe God's desire and purpose were (and still are) deeply at work within His church. This powerful notion resulted in my change of perspective as I found myself proclaiming, **"Wow! There's beauty in this!"**

I soon came to realize that this hidden beauty was otherworldly and had to be spiritually discerned. I remembered the times when Jesus spoke of shifts or a change in times and seasons, such as in John 4:21, "…From now on…" I couldn't help but wonder if we were in such a time. The thought that the world had been brought to a screeching halt and stopped dead in its tracks literally blew my mind! What could possibly be the reason for an epic worldwide shut-in where all the distractions of life were stripped away with nothing remaining but faith, family, and time to seek the Lord? As I marinated in John 4, I *saw* a link between the r- words in 2 Chronicles 7:14 and the s- words in John 4—namely, **spiritual** insight, **sensitivity,** and discernment of **seasons**! I was filled with fresh revelation as I considered the link between the chay-il-activated kingdom sons and daughters from Volume I, those on a journey of becoming who God intended in Volume II, and now in Volume III, God yearning for and seeking out those identified as True Worshippers in John 4! Considering the meaning of worship based on the original biblical text, which is to bow down as a servant or slave and to give oneself over to the power of another, it became clear that **the True Worshippers are those who live in a state of surrender to God.** These people are all one in the same, *chayil agents activated to serve the King's agenda!*

Another passage for the year 2020 was Acts 3:1-11, where Peter and John healed a lame man. Similar to the devastating situations confronting us in 2020, this man had a need that material goods, wealth, and possessions and anything born of man could not help. Whether one believes in God or not, there are times when only He can help! The lame man's need was present every time the temple was in use, yet no one, despite all their efforts, was able to make his situation better. All of that changed the day Peter and John passed by. They had an otherworldly and different approach. Paraphrased: "Every time people pass you, you receive some quantity of money, and your situation and life remain the same. We will not give you natural treasure. Instead, we will draw from the divine treasure that we carry, and you will be completely transformed. Now, in the name of Jesus, get up!" That day, the man got up and went into the temple on his own two feet! He was transformed, and Peter and John bore evidence, **Proof of Life**, that they were **carriers**!

At this point, I was clear about the message of Volume III. We, YHWH's Kingdom sons and daughters, as activated *chayil* agents, clear about our **Kingdom Identity** and on a journey of **Becoming Who He Knew**, are to rise from the dust of this great global shut-in full of faith and power! Having had unbroken fellowship in His presence for more than a year, we will witness **Carriers** manifesting in a powerful **Emergence of True Worshippers** who would serve to usher in God's great revival!

Chapter 1

KINGDOM ORIENTATION, KINGDOM IDENTITY, KING, KINGDOM, CHAYIL

Kingdom Orientation and Kingdom Identity

"Before I formed you in the womb I knew you
[and approved of you as My chosen instrument],
And before you were born I consecrated you [to
Myself as My own]; I have appointed you as a
prophet to the nations." Jeremiah 1:5 (AMP)

This Chayil Collection is based on the premise that we are cultivating our Kingdom Orientations and embracing our Kingdom Identities. An orientation determines our position, direction, and personal placement and allows us to establish functional boundaries for a specific posture and desired behavior. A Kingdom Orientation allows us *to see ourselves as assigned a primary role and function in God's divine, global Kingdom* (The

Christian's Kingdom Identity (volume 1). ***Thus, a Kingdom Orientation calls for a regular realignment of ideas and behavior based on a person's understanding of his or her specific assignment within the Kingdom of God.*** An identity is who a person really is, based on distinguishable qualities, traits, character, and personality. A ***Kingdom Identity*** is the true essence of a person's authentic self based on God's foreknowledge, will, and specific purpose. God has uniquely wired every person and placed purpose-specific deposits inside them. A Kingdom Identity is revealed by the Holy Spirit when people spend time in the Lord's presence and is discovered as His presence and glory are manifested through them. Similar to a natural identity, a kingdom identity is also recognized by distinguishable roles, functions, and fruit! ***A Kingdom Identity links a person's very existence to the King and His Kingdom and allows them to see themselves from a Kingdom perspective.***

The King and His Kingdom Agenda

God is King over the entire earth (Ps 47:2, 74:12)! As King, He rules a kingdom. A kingdom is the realm or domain governed by a principality. Since God is a Spirit, His Kingdom is His *spiritual* reign or authority, to which Jesus referred after being handed over to Pontius Pilate. When Pilate asked about His kingship, Jesus replied, "My kingdom is not of this world; if My kingdom were of this world, then would My servants fight, that I should not be delivered to the Jews: but now is My kingdom not from hence…Thou sayest that I am a king. To this end was I born, and for this cause came I into the world" (John 18:36-37). Jesus, very clear about His identity, never denied His kingship or divinity.

The tangible reality of *God's Kingdom realm is so important that Jesus only preached regarding the Kingdom, its principles, and its perspectives*: "And Jesus went about all Galilee, teaching in the synagogues, and preaching the gospel of the kingdom, and healing all manner of sickness and all manner of disease among the people" (Matt. 4:23). And again: "Now after John was put in prison, Jesus came into Galilee, preaching the gospel of the kingdom of God" (Mark 1:14). Thus, Jesus's teaching and preaching promoted the cultivation of a *Kingdom Orientation: embracing the reality of the Kingdom of God and the placement of your origin, purpose, and destiny within it.* This embrace promotes the discovery of your *Kingdom Identity: viewing your life from a kingdom aspect and yourself as one deliberately designed to facilitate the King's agenda.*

Jeremiah's call is a perfect example of someone who ultimately accepted his Kingdom Orientation and embraced his Kingdom Identity. His call occurred around the fall of Jerusalem (627-586 BC) and **depicts the Creator's attention to detail when depositing purpose into His creation.** <u>It is a clear example of a person living in alignment with his or her kingdom identity, which dictates a specific attitude, posture, and behavior complementary to one's assigned purpose.</u> Israel as a nation had a faith-based Kingdom Identity that was established at Mount Sinai (Ex. 19:5-25). They were to be His people, and He alone was to be their God. Israel was to be marked and identified by their complete obedience to YHWH, but in Jeremiah's day, their idolatry and broken covenant resulted in Babylon's invasion and the devastation of Jerusalem. Jeremiah's difficult destiny included announcing God's judgement and encouraging His people to surrender in hopes of restoration (33:4-9). At times, one's life-assignment can be grossly unappealing and difficult! Jeremiah's call to ministry (1:5) presents evidence of the placement of one's origin, purpose, and destiny— not just in the physical world but within the Kingdom of God itself. It also introduces the notion of God knowing and distinguishing someone before he or she even exists, establishing the premise of an individual's life-journey of Becoming Who God Knew (volume 2).

Before I <u>formed</u> you in the womb I <u>knew</u> you,
before you were born I <u>set you apart</u>; I <u>appointed</u>
you as a prophet to the nations.
Jeremiah 1:5 (NIV)

You will notice throughout these volumes some analysis of specific words in the original text to provide a richer meaning and a more thorough understanding. Having completed such for the underlined verbs above affords a rough translation for Jeremiah 1:5.

Verb	Hebrew	Translation
form	*yatser* (yaw-tsar)	establish / frame from foresight / previous thought
knew	*yada* (yaw-dah)	to have had regard for, to have fed / cared / provided for specific to nurturing geared to one's uniqueness (based on foresight)
consecrate	*qadash* (qaw-dash)	give / set / designated / placed in a unique roll / function
appoint	*nathan* (naw-than)	give / put / establish, make to become, wired, given to the earth as

Rough Hebrew Translation Jeremiah 1:5

Before I <u>framed you from foresight</u>, I <u>had regard for you</u>, carefully <u>nurturing your specific uniqueness</u>; before you were born, I <u>set, designated, and placed you in a unique function and position</u>; I <u>established you, made you to become, and gave you to the earth as</u> a prophet to the nations.

God was hands-on in nurturing Jeremiah's overall well-being *before he was born*! God, the Alpha and Omega, orchestrated his end from the beginning and was completely committed to his lifelong journey! It highlights God's sovereign involvement in the everyday affairs of human life. **Jeremiah's life was NEVER without meaning or purpose, and neither is yours or mine.**

Kingdom Agenda: Let There Be Light!

In the beginning when God created the heavens and the earth, the earth was a formless void and darkness covered the face of the deep, while a wind from God swept over the face of the waters. **Then God said, "Let there be light," and there was light.** *And God saw that the light was good; and God separated the light from the darkness. God called the light Day, and the darkness he called Night. And there was*

evening and there was morning, the first day.
(Gen. 1:1-5 NRSV)

The King's calculated actions align with a pre-planned agenda **to cancel darkness**, the "chaos or negation" (Isa. 45:7, 60:2) that opposes His goodness and blessings on creation. [1] The effect of darkness results in a lesser state of glory than the Creator-King's intended desire for His creation. On the contrary, Light is the force that works in accordance with God's divine provision for the overall well-being of creation. Light results in creation's highest level of glory, brilliance, and beauty, seen in its expression of its predetermined capacity and fullest potential. This Chayil Collection submits that one of the first things God created meta-phorically depicts His ultimate worldwide agenda for all times: *Let There Be Light!* YHWH's agenda to cancel darkness with light involved recruiting His people as carriers of His light, a topic we will pick up in chapter 3 (Gen. 12:1-3, 18:18, 28:14). These would affect a 3D blessing— spirit, soul, and body— for all nations.

---

[1] Celine Vieria, "The Mission of the Servant," *Missio Aposolica* 22.1 (May 2014): 131-136.

Chayil

The King
The right hand of the Lord is exalted!
The right hand of the Lord performs with **valor**
(*chayil*)! (Ps. 118:16 BSB)

David
Behold, I have seen the son of Jesse the
Bethlehemite, who is skillful in playing, a man
of **valor** (*ish chayil*), a man of war, prudent in
speech, and a man of good presence, and the
LORD is with him (1 Sam. 16:18 ESV).

Proverbial Woman
A woman of **valour** (*eshet chayil*) who can find?
For her price is far above rubies (Prov. 31:10 JPS
Tanakh 1917).

לַיַח , *chayil* (ka-yil), is a Hebrew masculine
noun, which has among its many translations
"strength," "power," "valor," "army," and "host."
Its root form occurs 224 times in the Old Testament,
mostly in military terms such as valiant (Ps. 60:12)
and army (Ps. 33:16 NASB). The Proverbs 31:10
form of *chayil* occurs 136 times and is translated
as "capable" (NRSV), "noble" (NIV), "excellent"
(NIRV), and "accomplished" (TLV). *Chayil* may
also be translated as "force" (2 Chron. 17:12 KJV)

and "wealth or substance" (Ps. 49:6). Additionally, Brown, Driver, and Briggs render *chayil* as "ability," often involving but never replaced with terms indicating "moral worth" (298). Despite this, most English translations of *chayil* referencing women, like Proverbs 31:10, use a word that is different from this traditional understanding.

Chayil may stand alone, indicating "strength" (Prov. 31:10), "army" (2 Kings 25:5), "wealth," "efficiency," or "might." It may also be combined in a phrase such as *ish chayil*, man of valor (2 Chron. 28:6), or *ben chayil*, son of might (1 Chron. 11:22).[2] As you have probably noticed, *chayil* is an all-inclusive (spirit, soul, and body), multifaceted term, a jewel of truth. It speaks to the nature of God in all His fullness and ultimately to the true identity of His sons and daughters, powerful warriors who I refer to as super-natural heroes activated for a common Cause: Let There Be Light!

For an abbreviated list of *chayil* men and women in the Old Testament, please review *Volume 1: The Christian's Kingdom Identity*. Worth mentioning is the fact that in 1 Samuel 14:52, King Saul would only enlist an *ish chayil* (man of valor, strength, or war) in his army, obviously aware of this caliber of warrior who would complete his assigned

---

[2] George V. Wigram, *Englishman's Hebrew Concordance of the Old Testament* (Massachusetts: Hendrickson Publishers, 1995), *chayil*

task at any cost. Is it any surprise then that the King of Glory would summon an elite force of His very own *chayil* agents, giving them a mission to advance His Kingdom agenda all over the earth? While the Bible contains many different stories featuring an *ish chayil* (man of valor) and fewer featuring an *eshet chayil* (woman of valor), not all of them were activated to serve YHWH's efforts.

The first volume's focus on David and the Proverbs 31 woman sought to analyze and extrapolate information regarding their motivation, attitude, and actions in an effort to establish a type of *chayil agency* (see below). Volume II used this agency to identify other biblical characters, some without the *chayil* epithet, who exemplified the same attributes and activation for service. This *chayil* agency further facilitates the reader's personal journey of discovering his or her kingdom identity and aligning with their individual process of *chayil* activation. Now, let's examine the source of *chayil*.

Chayil Agency from
The Christian's Kingdom Identity: Vol I.

Shows human beings....

as supernatural heroes activated for a common cause
who link their identity, cause, and ability to God
capable of defeating their adversaries, either alone or as part of an elite troop
who are worthy and noble
as people of excellence
as selfless risk-takers
who are mission-minded
who center their efforts around the bigger picture for the greater good of all
who perform great feats
who are trustworthy, reliable, and capable
as leaders placed in positions of power and influence
who are studious and hard-working
who are winners and will complete tasks at any cost

God's Old Testament names indicate how He manifested Himself and how His presence was perceived by those who experienced it. Some of these names began with El, a generic term meaning God. In particular, in Abraham's time, various names described many facets of the same God.[3] Judaism, unlike many other religions, has one divine name that is held in the heart: YHWH, a name too holy to utter directly, was pronounced "Adonai," meaning *Lord*, before the third century B.C.[4] *YHWH* is the name God used when He made a covenant with Moses (Ex. 3:6). *YHWH*, "Ehyeh as-her Ehyeh," is translated "I will be, I could be, I might be, I may be, or I may become, **Whoever** I will be, could be, might be, may be, or may become" (3:14).[5] **It is here that God explained that the cries of His people had "come up to Him" and that He "was come down" to rescue them through Moses, His human deliverer** (Ex. 3:1-15). The principle shown is, whenever God-given freedom, justice, and equality are threatened, the God of Valor, the Warrior God, becomes what is crucial in breaking the chains of oppression and obtaining victory. *YHWH* then is "the God of Potentialities," the "God of Possibilities," the "Living God of *Becoming* and *Transforming*," the "One who can liberate them from bondage in Egypt." [6] Hence, the name *YHWH* summons "the

---

[3] Allen S. Maller, "Unique and Shared Names of God in Islam and Judaism," *Journal of Ecumenical Studies* 49.4 (Fall 2014): 647.

[4] Ibid.

[5] Ibid, 647.

[6] Ibid.

One who brings potentials into existence" by any means necessary,[7] most often **through a human male or female deliverer of His choice.**

Another early name of God, *El Shaddai* or Almighty God, also indicates God's military nature. "Almighty God" exalts Him above every other god to a position having no equal and no rival. *El Shaddai* was inaccurately translated into Greek as *Pantokrator*, all-powerful or omnipotent, instead of "The God who is sufficient"[8] or "God alone is enough." Even still, we can how these names of God coincide with the translations of *chayil*: able, capable, full, most mighty, almighty, or valiant.

Chayil is an all-inclusive term which expresses the fullness of the glory of God. Though the name *El Chayil*, the God of Valor, is not used, the persona of a warrior God is thoroughly supported in the scriptures (Ps. 104:14 and 118:15, among many others). Psalm 24:8 portrays God as a warrior, owner of the entire universe and all it contains, describing Him as "the King of Glory, Lord strong and mighty, mighty in battle." The *God of Valor* moves throughout the earth with a strategic plan, thwarting the plans of the evil one against His creation. Psalm 118:16 states, "The right hand of the LORD is exalted; The right hand of the LORD does

---

[7] Ibid, 649.

[8] Ibid.

valiantly." Right hand, יָמִין (*yamin*), is an instrument of deliverance (Ex. 15:6, 12); it opposes enemies (Ps. 21:9), distributes blessings (Ps. 48:11), and is also used in divine oaths (62:8). Certainly, the Lord of Hosts is an elite warrior!

David, the slayer of giants, proclaimed God as his source of *chayil* in 2 Samuel 22:33: "It is God who arms me with *chayil*, and makes my way secure!" I love the way it reads in the NIV: "God is my *chayil*…!" Psalms confirms God as David's *chayil* source and activator: "It is God who arms me with strength (*chayil*) and keeps my way secure" (Ps. 18:32 NIV). Though a modern trend is to show David as a force within his own right, David gave all the credit to YHWH: "You armed me with strength [*chayil*] for battle; you humbled my adversaries before me" (Ps. 18:39 NIV); "Through God we shall do valiantly (have *chayil*), and it is He who will tread down our adversaries" (Ps. 60:12 NASB).

Psalms continues to confirm the God of Valor in *chayil* references like 84:7, which shows that *chayil* is gained in the presence of YHWH: "They go from strength (*chayil*) to strength. *Every one of them* appears before God in Zion." God is reiterated as the source of *chayil* in 108:13 (NIV): "With God we will gain the victory, and He will trample down our enemies." Notice the use of the preposition *with*. Jesus said, "Apart from me you can do nothing" (John 15:6), **indicating that a relationship with Him is crucial for the human deliverer.** There is rejoicing due to the activities of *El Chayil*: "The sound of joyful shouting and salvation is in the tents of the righteous; The right hand of the LORD does valiantly [or has brought us *chayil*]" (118:15 NASB), and again, "The right hand of the LORD is exalted; The right hand of the LORD does valiantly" (118:16 NASB). God Himself activates *chayil* in His servants.

The voices of our day allege that our activated qualities and attributes find their origin within us. However, like David, **the *chayil* agent affirms God as his or her *chayil* source.** Ephesians 3:20 confirms this truth: "Now unto Him who is able to do exceedingly, abundantly, above all we ask or think, *according to the power* [chayil] *that works* [or is activated] *in you*." Regardless of one's level of education, socio-economic status, or networking ability, for *chayil agents,* activation is only obtained as a result of encountering YHWH! *Chayil*-activated agents have a resounding battle cry that includes a preposition linking their ability to God! "*With* God, all things are possible" (Matt. 19:26). "Remain *in* me and I *in* you, and ye can ask what ye will" (John 15:7). Never forget your Source. Never forget the prepositions. Now, let's move ahead to discover the connection between *chayil* agents and true worshippers!

Chapter II

THE EMERGENCE OF TRUE WORSHIPPERS

"Yet a time is coming and has now come when the true worshippers will worship the Father in Spirit and in truth, for they are the kind of worshipers the Father seeks. 24 God is Spirit, and His worshipers must worship in the Spirit and in truth." John 4:23-24

At the start of the 2020 quarantine, due to the COVID-19 pandemic, the importance of clarity of vision, not 20/20 vision but 2020 vision, became quite apparent. In other words, activated spiritual senses were required to rightly discern the major global paradigm shifts that were occurring on many levels. There was no aspect of living that wasn't impacted by the pandemic and resulting quarantine. Everything was shut down, and we were in a divine shut-in. Nations around the world had all been stripped of all distractions, that which is tailor-made to draw one away from his or her desired course or path, often resulting in diminished productivity and growth. Additionally, things we thought we couldn't live without were now gone, including places of worship. Many wondered, how will we continue to worship? It was quite common to hear various people expressing how much they missed "going to church" and their "corporate worship experiences."

Worship

I mean, I get it! Human beings were created to worship, and thus, we have a proclivity and tendency to do so. Revelations 4:11, John 1:3, and Colossians 1:16 (TPT) support this notion of God creating human beings to worship and glorify God:

> *You are worthy, our Lord and God, to receive glory, honor, and power, for You created all things, and for Your pleasure they were created and exist. Revelation 4:11*

> *For in Him was created the universe of things, both in the heavenly realm and on the earth, all that is seen and all that is unseen. Every seat of power, realm of government, principality, and authority-it all*

exists through Him and for His purpose! Colossians 1:16

And through His creative inspiration this Living Expression made all things, for nothing has existence apart from him! John 1:3

As one who considers the Word of God as the ultimate Truth, I looked to the Scriptures for the true meaning of worship. In Hebrew, worship is **abad** and translates as to serve, work, to become slave or servant to, to obey, to be enslaved, and to keep in service as a bondman. As seen, biblical worship has very little to do with singing, clapping, or dancing, though these acts stream from a heart of worship. Instead, **worship is to figuratively bow down and symbolizes the act of willfully giving oneself over to another—living in a continued state of surrender as a vassal or servant; one who is submitted to and subordinate to another.** In Romans 12:2 (NLT), Paul agrees:

> *And so, dear brothers and sister, I plead with you to **give your bodies (selves) to God** because of all He has done for you Let them be a **living and holy sacrifice-the kind He will find acceptable. This is truly the way to worship Him.***

Many versions translate this as true and proper worship or reasonable service, indicating that this type of sacrifice is an obligation. Several Bible verses command, *"Worship the Lord and serve Him only"* (Ex. 8:20, 9:13, 10:24; Deut. 6:13, 10:8, 12, 20; 13:4; 1 Chron. 28:9; 1 Kings 25:53; Josh. 10:6, 22:5, 24:14-15, 24; 1 Sam. 7:3, 12:14, 20, 24; 26:19; 2 Sam. 12:20; Isa. 56:6; Zeph. 3:9; Matt. 4:10; Luke 4:8), while more than several hundred declare, *"Worship the Lord."* **One major 2020 shift was a shift in our perspective of worship.** In light of this new understanding, a specific time, place, or group of people have very little to do with one's worship, which is living in a state of surrender to the will of God. God was after something specific in 2020, and we were to align with His desire and give it to Him!

I submit that even those who boast in not believing in God have probably given themselves over to some other influence, which, in essence, is worship. The fact is that human beings are bound to worship something or someone! One of Satan's ultimate goals is to deceive God's people into worshipping another. Exodus 34:14 (NLT) is sober a reminder: "You must worship no other gods, for the Lord, whose very name is Jealous, is a God who is jealous about His relationship with you." We must live in bold defiance to the tendency to bow to any influence other than God's! Let's look at John 4, where Jesus described this shift in perspective of worship.

John 4

This narrative is filled with timely content as it speaks to systemic racism, extreme prejudice, gender inequalities, social injustice, religious biases, and more. As I meditated in John 4 throughout the year of 2020, the messages of the Holy Spirit cries within it rang loud and clear! Jesus's mission was to break down the walls of division so that there would be no schisms between Jew and Greek, male and female, and others. May we hear the Holy Spirit's call for spiritual insight, sensitivity, and discernment of the seasons, which will facilitate our personal alignment with the King's demand!

This narrative opens with Jesus's announcement that He was going to defy religious and societal conventions and go to a place where the Samaritans (considered outsiders) lived. This longstanding divide between the Jews and the Samaritans was due to the Jews regarding the Samaritans as unclean or half-breeds because they were mixed with multiple ethnicities. As mentioned earlier, both groups believed in the same God and read the same Scripture, but there were differences in styles and places of worship. The Jews would go out of their way to avoid the

Samaritans. But this was the opposite of what God wanted Jesus, His only begotten Son, to do, as John 4;4 (NKJV) says, "But He needed to go through Sararia." The word "need" is loaded here, indicating more than the shortest distance or easiest path. No, this trip had been divinely established and written in the heavenly script. It was God's will. Have you ever felt strongly that God was leading you to do something that was beyond the framework of your circle and could possibly be frowned upon by those whose opinions matter?

Jesus was sent on a mission to minister to the life of one person, a female, who lived in the wrong place and was born to the wrong people. As previously mentioned, not only were her gender and ethnicity problematic, but so were her social status, lifestyle and even her neighborhood. Yet, God's love for this woman caused Him to send her Jesus! God's plan included her personal one-on-one encounter with Jesus! This passage appears to highlight the kingdom significance of one ordinary person, perhaps something we've forgotten due to the desire for more likes to build a following. Let's face it, most speakers enjoy a packed auditorium or large crowd, but here we have a call to align with what makes heaven rejoice: "In the same way, I tell you, there is rejoicing in the presence of the angels of God over one sinner who repents" (Luke 15:10 NIV).

This Samaritan woman was minding her business and doing what was customary, drawing water from the well. Jesus, a Jewish rabbi, showed up, took a seat, and spoke to her, "Give Me a drink." This smells like a setup! Jesus was there to break traditional barriers and completely transform this woman's life. The Samaritan woman asked Jesus, "How is it that you being a Jew would ask me to draw water for you?" In other words, "Our kind don't usually converse."

Jesus now took the opportunity to fulfill His assignment: **"If you knew who I am and the Gift God has for you, you would ask me for a drink."** Notice how Jesus spoke from a spiritual perspective regarding His kingdom identity: "If you knew who I am, you would know that I have what you need…" The problem here was one of spiritual insight. The woman was completely unaware of Jesus's identity and did not recognize the authentic presence of Christ the Messiah.

Again, from a natural perspective having their religion, lineage, and history in mind, she asked, "Are you greater than our father Jacob who dug this well? He drank from it himself." Surely, no one is greater than He! The woman lacked spiritual sensitivity as she was unable to move beyond the systemic divide and the natural order of things.

Jesus, who continued to speak from a kingdom aspect, moved further in to release His divine deposit, at the same time, divine activation was taking place in her. "The water you give, will only satisfy temporarily. But I have living water or the water of Life. Once you drink of this water, you will never thirst again!"

She sarcastically exclaimed, "My goodness, please give me this special water. Then I won't have to keep coming here for more." Dominated by her natural senses, she completely missed the point!

Finally, Jesus revealed His power and gift to her when He asked, "Go call your husband and come back." After she honestly told Jesus that she didn't have one, He offered her Proof of Divine Life in His response, affirming that she was telling the truth, that she had had five husbands, and that the man she currently was with was not her husband. At this point, she was more interested in their conversation and believed that Jesus was a religious man, a prophet.

She then insisted, as if this one thing had always bothered her and she wanted to know which was politically correct, "Please tell me this one thing. You Jews say that one must go to Jerusalem, the holy place, to worship God. Our people say we must worship here on this mountain. **Which place is the proper place to worship?**"

Here, Jesus revealed a major shift as He addressed the third problem, discerning the god-season, "From this time forward, worship-ping the Father will not be a matter of the right place, but a matter of the right heart. For God is a Spirit, and he longs, searches, yearns, seeks, looks for those who will adore Him in the realm of the Spirit and in Truth." Jesus designated a shift, fore-telling of a time which includes the manifestation of the kingdom often described by the **already, but not yet principle,** "…a time will come, and now is…" This new season is a time when Kingdom demands render the religious and conventional traditions null and void, like places and styles of worship. He further explained that worship, the giving of oneself over to another as a servant or the living in a state of submission to another, is not a matter of when or where but of the heart. Wow! **The state of one's heart informs one's service-worship.** Jesus communicated that God longs for, yearns, and seeks after those whose ser-vice-worship is flowing from the right heart. It reminds me of the answer to a question in Psalms 24, "Who shall ascend into the hill of the Lord? Or who shall stand in His holy place? He that hath cleans hands and a pure heart; who hath not lifted up his soul to vanity, nor sworn deceitfully" (Ps. 24:3-4). Here, Jesus presented a Kingdom aspect of worship. **Worship, one's state of surrender or submission to God, may be expressed in song or symbolized by a physical bowing down, but**

these acts in and of themselves do not consti-
tute authentic worship. Clapping of the hands
and leaping for joy are not necessarily acts motivated by a heart that is given over to God. Jesus
announced that God was looking for those who
adore Him to the point of living in a state of consistent surrender to Him in the Spirit realm and in
Truth, far beyond outward demonstration. In fact,
many versions of this verse (24) contain the word,
"...**must** worship in the Spirit and in truth," indicating that this is only type of worship that God
finds acceptable or pleasing, as in Romans 12:2.

Jesus continued to demonstrate spiritual
insight, sensitivity, and discernment of seasons
and moved in for her ultimate breakthrough. After
the woman explained her religious understanding
of the Messiah and His coming, Jesus spoke with
powerful authority and declared, "I, the one
speaking to you-I am He." At this point, the disciples returned and were shocked to find Jesus
speaking with a woman because this was quite
unconventional. The woman, by now completely
ignited by her encounter with the Lord, went to
town and told the people to come see a man who
told her everything she had ever done. "Could this
be the Messiah?" They went to meet Him.

As a result of her encounter with the Lord, not
only were her spiritual problems addressed, but
she was completely transformed and activated by

His powerful presence, and in typical *chayil* agent fashion, she became an effective witness and a true worshipper who invited many others to experience the same! As seen with *chayil* agents, it wasn't enough for her to experience YHWH's deliverance; she wanted others to as well, causing her to serve the King's agenda! This dialogue prophetically speaks to the global Body of Christ and serves as a call for activation and alignment, which is to commence in a great revival. Like the Samaritan woman, having spent time, an entire quarantine, in the presence of the Lord, there are those who hear the call to arise in a new state of surrender. The Holy Spirit has poured out the Water of Life on His sons and daughters, His *chayil* agents. Each *ish chayil* and *eschet chayil* is to be numbered among powerful **Carriers** of His presence, manifesting in an anointed **Emergence of True Worshippers.**

Chapter III

CARRIERS OF A DIVINE DEPOSIT

"We are like common clay jars that **carry this glorious treasure within***, so that the extraordinary overflow of power will be seen as God's, not ours."* 2 Corinthians 4:7 (TPT)

The Light. The Word. The Life. The Power.

The previous chapters fill us with joy as the Father's love, desire, and selection of us are reaffirmed! We are equipped with revelation knowledge powerful enough to defeat the enemy's attempts of discouragement, depression, and even suicide as we learn that our existence is no mistake and we are loaded with divine purpose, potential, and capacity. In fact, we are not alive to forge out our own way, but we were born to advance God's Kingdom Agenda, which existed long before we did! What a source of encouragement it is when we come to understand that we have a part to play in a Cause much greater than our own, which has an origin that is otherworldly and benefits that are eternal. Now, let's take a look in the Book of Beginnings, Genesis, at God's original plan for human beings in an effort to understand why His Kingdom sons and daughters become carriers.

> *Now the Lord said to Abram, go from your country and your kindred and your father's house to the land that I will show you. I will make you a great nation, and I will bless you, and make your name great, **so that you will be a blessing**. I will bless those who bless you, and the one who curses you I will curse; **and in you all the families of the earth shall be blessed.** Genesis 12:1-3 (NRSV)*

As stated in previous volumes, God's desire for an intimate, ongoing relationship with human beings was instituted in the Garden of Eden with Adam and Eve. Throughout Scripture, **God goes to great lengths to use His creation as *carriers of the Light of His presence* so that the peoples of the earth could enter into relationship with Him as His children through faith.**[9] The great blessing mentioned in verse 3 is intimacy with YHWH, <u>demonstrated by and extended through His own people.</u> In "The Wealth of the Nations

---

[9] Ibid.

Shall Come to You," C. Jones describes how Isaiah 60 opens with the entire world lying "shrouded in deep darkness, when suddenly, YHWH's glorious presence dawns upon Zion."[10] As the dispersed returned home when God restored Jerusalem, Zion was to be *the single point of light in a world flooded with darkness.*[11] I submit that this prophetic portrait of Zion as the single source of Light in a dark world is an accurate depiction even in our day!

> *1. Rise up in splendor and **be radiant**, for your light has dawned, and Yahweh's glory now **streams from you**!*
>
> *2. Look carefully! Darkness blankets the earth, and thick gloom covers the nations, **but Yahweh arises upon you** and the brightness of his glory **appears over you**! Isaiah 60:1-2 (TPT)*

Dr. Donna Raynal brilliantly depicts the light as salvific acts of God through His people.[12] In the passage above, YHWH's glorious light is upon His people, flows from His people, and appears

---

[10] Christopher M. Jones, "The Wealth of Nations Shall Come to You: Light, Tribute, and Implacement in Isaiah 60," *Vestus Testamentum* 4 (2014): 621.

[11] Walter J. Burghardt, "From Gloom to Glory: Expository Articles," *Interpretation* 44.4 (October 1990): 397.

[12] Donna Desarro-Raynal, "Between Texts and Sermons: Isaiah 60:1-6," *Interpretation* 67.1 (January 2013): 61-63.

over His people. This encounter with God's powerful presence transforms them, and they become activated, effective witnesses, carriers of God's blessing and glory. John's testimony (John 1) also bears witness of this Light! "In the beginning…" marks the start of time and further shows that the Word, which is Jesus, was already present with God and in fact IS God. Through Jesus, the Word, all things came into being. John further states that in Jesus Christ is Life, and **this Life** is **the Light of all people** (John 1:4). John confirmed what Isaiah said above—the Light of all people, Jesus, shines in darkness *but is never overcome by it*. Instead, **Light cancels darkness every time, and the blessing for all families of the earth is inclusion in this Great Let There Be Light Campaign!**

This intertwined theme of the **Word** and the **Light** is repeated throughout the Scriptures, and as carriers, we must see the significance and understand the urgent need for both! (Ps. 119:105, 130). **Darkness represents all that would cancel the effect of the Word of God in the lives of human beings:** "The people that walked in darkness have seen a great Light: they that dwell in the shadow of death, upon them hath the Light shined" (Isa. 9:2). This Light is a power source for freedom, guidance, vision, and joyful living! The glory experienced is the manifested presence of the Kingdom of God, just as Jesus said in Matthew 12:28 (KJV), "But if it is by the Spirit of God that I cast out demons, then the Kingdom of God has come upon you." Every time the Light cancels darkness and a life is transformed by God's power, it is evidence of the presence of His Kingdom, which is, as stated above, **already but not yet**.

Everywhere we go, there's a kingdom demand or expectation for activated carriers of the presence of YHWH to continue the ministry of Jesus Christ on earth, loosing the bands of wickedness, undoing the heavy burdens, letting the oppressed go free, and breaking every yoke (Luke 4:18-19). Luke picked up Jesus's purpose and ministry found in Isaiah, "He has anointed me to proclaim good news to the poor. He has sent me to proclaim freedom for the prisoners and recovery of sight (restorers of vision) for the blind, to set the oppressed free, to proclaim the year of the Lord's favor (Isa. 61:1-2). I submit that this is always the outcome in the lives of people every time the presence of the King is manifested!

1 In the beginning the Word already existed. The Word was with God, and the Word was God. 2 He existed in the beginning with God. 3 ***God created everything through Him, and nothing was created except through Him****. 4* ***The Word gave life to*** *everything that was created, and His life brought light to everyone. 5 The light shines in the darkness, and the darkness can never extinguish it.* 9. *The one who is the true Light, who gives Light to everyone, was coming into the world. 10 He came to the very world He created, but the world did not recognize Him. 11. He came to His own people, and even they rejected Him. 12 But to all who believed Him and accepted Him, He gave the right to become children of God. 13* <u>*They are reborn-not with a physical birth resulting from human passion or plan, but a birth that comes from God.*</u> *14 So the Word became human and made His home among us. He was full of unfailing love and faithfulness. And we have seen his glory, the glory of the Father's one and only Son. John 1:1-5, 9-14 (NLT)*

Here we find the same problems identified in John 4—**spiritual insight**, **sensitivity,** and **discernment of seasons**. Jesus, God wrapped in flesh, entered the world He created and was not recognized. John, having had a divine encounter in his mother's womb (a miracle), was activated to become an effective witness. "God sent a man, John the Baptist, 7 to tell about the light so that everyone might believe because of his testimony (John 1:6-7). John was able to discern the season of the manifested Messiah, Light, and knew who He was. Yet the Scriptures report that Jesus was rejected by His own. Verse 12 is where we carriers come in, "But as many as received Him, to them gave He the power (right, authority) to become the sons (children) of God, even to them that believe on His name" (KJV). Not only are we carriers of Jesus, the Son, but we carry His **authority** and **power** as well! We are children of the King, hence, Kingdom sons and daughters! The implication is when the Word or Son is received and rebirth takes place, the divine Life and Light of the Son are also received. The Holy Spirit activates Christ's divine attributes in human beings, enabling the workings of various gifts and abilities. That's why 2 Corinthians 4:7 says, "…so that the extraordinary overflow of power will be seen as God's, not ours." We are equipped for service as carriers of His **Life**, **Word**, **Power,** and **Light,** which cancels the darkness that obscures the vision of humans (spiritual insight), blocks guidance (discernment of seasons), brings chaos and confusion (sensitivity), and blankets them with the heaviness of gloom and despair (Isa. 60)! The Word brings Light, which is the power that extinguishes darkness, causing Life in creation to explode with God's predetermined glory! Light brings clarity of purpose and guidance, affording individuals the opportunity to align with God's will and purpose and function as He intended.

Why are we carriers? Because the enemy's greatest weapon is darkness! Darkness wars against the effects of the Word by inhibiting creation's ability to align with God's will, its divine capacity. **Darkness simply cannot be tolerated!** But never fear! God's supernatural heroes, His sons and daughters, His activated *chayil* agents, are sent out as modern-day deliverers. Whenever the presence of darkness negatively impacts creation, the Scriptures clearly depict God coming to its rescue by sending a human deliverer when His people cry for help. Carriers, true worshippers given to the King's service, have a never-ending prayer in their hearts: "Father, allow me to be a source of Light today! May I extend Your kingdom agenda by canceling darkness!"

Chapter IV.

LIFELINE: INTIMACY & WORSHIP

"'My food,' said Jesus, 'is to do the will of Him who sent Me and to finish His work.'"
John 4:34 (NIV)

God's plan, purpose, and desire are the vehicles of worship, the **service-worship** of the true worshipper. We read in Chapter 2 that sincere or true worshippers live in service to God's will, which is their worship to Him. Jesus modeled the True Worshippers' **service-worship** to God and its powerful results. In John 4:34, He declared that the will of God is food, which not only provides nourishment and substance for spiritual-life but brings delight, satisfaction, and fulfillment. In other words, **God's will gave Him life!** Here we find another kingdom principle that is key in the lives of true worshippers. **Living in worship to the King, which requires intimacy and alignment with His will, is the lifeline for** *chayil* **agents.** Is it any wonder then why the enemy of purpose consistently makes attempts to deceive God's servants into living self-sufficiently, void of abiding in the vine? Satan's goal is to get God's people to break fellowship with Him by any means necessary. He wants to kill, steal, and destroy their lifeline.

A lifeline is something used as a way of rescue or life-saving. It provides a means of escape from a difficult situation. It is also used to keep contact with the Life-Saver (Hello!), should a potentially dangerous situation arise. **A lifeline is indispensable to the maintenance of life.** In John 15, Jesus used the analogy of the vine (Him) and the branch (you and me) as He taught that remaining in Him or attached to Him is vital to our spiritual life and that bearing much fruit and glorifying God is contingent on this connection. He also emphasized that it is impossible to do God's will, which is our Spirit-food, without remaining within this connection, "…apart from me, you can do nothing" (15:5). Kingdom language and spiritual principles often do not make sense in the natural realm. Paul explained this in 1 Corinthians 2:14 (NIV), "The person without the Spirit does not accept the things that come from the Spirit of God but considers them foolishness, and cannot understand them because they are discerned only through the Spirit." **Jesus proclaimed that His living in service to God's will, which is worship,**

provides nourishment, satisfaction, and fulfill-ment for our spiritual lives. In this light, **Worship is a Lifeline!**

Worship as a lifeline puts a new spin on Philippians 4:13 (AMP),

> *I can do all things [which He has called me to do] through Him who strengthens and empowers me [to fulfill His purpose—I am self-sufficient in Christ's sufficiency; I am ready for anything and equal to anything through Him who infuses me with inner strength and confident peace.]*

True Worshippers, or *chayil* agents, know where to go to receive strength. They have an unending supply of help and support for the Maker of heaven and earth is their Source. The infusion of inner strength, or times of refreshing, flows from His very presence (Acts 3:19). **Hosting the presence of the Holy Spirit is a way of life for these activated carriers as intimacy fuels their worship and worship gives them life.** Whatever their task, or life-assignment, the True Worshipper knows and believes that it is possible.

The vehicle for intimacy with the Lord is the Word of God. It provokes and promotes commu-nication with Him, which is a key component to authentic intimacy in any relationship. In fact, true worshippers hold God's Word as the ultimate source of truth, and in it, God's plan and will for mankind is revealed. In order to know and understand God and hear His voice, we must know, meditate, and saturate ourselves in His Word. True Worshippers must defy the prevalent lie that the Word of God is outdated and has diminished capacity in this present time. Hebrews 4:12 declares, "For the Word of God is alive and powerful. It is sharper than the sharpest two-edged sword, cutting between the soul and spirit, between joint and marrow. It exposes our innermost thoughts and desires" (NLT). The Word of God is no ordinary book; it provides clarity and discernment, capable of revealing one's motives and intentions. Don't forget that Jesus, Himself, is the Word of God! As such, the Word provides guidance, "Thy Word is a lamp unto my feet and a Light unto my path" (Ps. 119:105).

An intimate relationship with the Lord is directly linked to entrance into His Kingdom! The parable of the wise and foolish virgins beautifully depicts such importance (Matt. 25 TPT). It's important to note that **Oil** in the Scriptures is a metaphor for the presence of the Holy Spirit, who brings us **revelation** of the Word of God and **power** for ministry (NRSV notes). Hence, we are also carriers of His Oil!

*When my coming draws near, heaven's kingdom realm can be compared to ten maidens who took their **oil lamps** and went outside to meet the bridegroom and his bride. 2–4 Five of them were **foolish and ill-prepared**, for **they took no extra oil for their lamps**. Five of them were **wise**, for **they took flasks of olive oil with their lamps**. 5 When the bridegroom didn't come when they expected, **they all grew drowsy and fell asleep**. 6 Then suddenly, in the middle of the night, they were **awakened** by the shout "Get up! The bridegroom is here! Come out and have **an encounter** with him!" 7 So all the girls got up and trimmed their lamps. 8 But **the foolish ones were running out of oil**, so they said to the five wise ones, "Share your oil with us, because **our lamps are going out**!" 9 **"We can't,"** they replied. "We don't have enough for all of us. You'll have to <u>go and buy some</u> for yourselves!" 10 While the five girls were <u>out buying oil</u>, **the bride-groom appeared**. Those who were **ready and waiting** were **escorted inside with him** and the wedding party to enjoy the feast. And then the door was locked. 11 Later, the five foolish girls came running up to the door and pleaded, **"Lord, Lord, let us come in!"** 12 But he called back, "Go away! <u>Do I know you? **I can assure you, I don't even know you!**</u>" 13 That is the*

*reason you should always **stay awake and
be alert**, because you don't know the day or
the hour when the Bridegroom will appear.
Matthew 25:1-13 (TPT)*

<u>Jesus compared a major Kingdom event, His
return, to half of the population in this parable
being considered foolish because they had not
committed to the process of receiving a continual
flow of Oil from the Source.</u> This priceless Oil
determined the outcome of their destiny and ultimately where they would spend eternity. The wise
girls were deemed so due to their honoring the Oil,
considering it precious, something they could not
exist without. Therefore, they took care to **guard
their supply of Oil**, **ensuring that they would
never run out.** The problem in the parable is that
the event for which they needed Oil was delayed.
The Bridegroom did not return in a timely fashion,
and they all lost focus. Often, a delay in the arrival
of the promise is a test of faith. During the waiting
process, the last thing one should do is lose focus
and change their posture, position, or placement
(Kingdom Orientation). All the maidens became
drowsy and fell asleep, which is indicative of a lack
of vigilance and keenness and is quite dangerous.
The Bible is loaded with warnings regarding a
state of being "at ease" or "asleep." "Woe to them
that are at ease in Zion…" (Amos 6:1). When the

young ladies least expected it, in the dead of night, in a season that appeared to be one of decreased fruitfulness, when nothing much was happening and their needs were the greatest, the Bridegroom returned. There was a shout, an invitation to come and have an **encounter with Him**. It is then that the foolish young women realized that they were running out of Oil. The foolish maidens asked the wise ones to share some Oil with them, and they uttered two of the most powerful yet disturbing words a Christian could ever hear, **"We can't!"** Their reason: "We don't have enough to go around, and if we share our Oil, we too will run out, and running out of Oil is not an option. It's too precious and costly and determines our eternal destination!" **Running out of Oil is not an option!** So, the unwise young women went to the store to buy oil. We must make mention that the store may have some oil, but it is not The **Oil**. It's as if the ladies had been forced to settle for a counterfeit. Perhaps this strange or wrong oil is why the Bridegroom responded, *"I don't know you!"*

This meeting is no ordinary one. In the Greek, this noun signifies the action of "having a meeting" or "an encounter." It was time to be transformed, healed, strengthened, refreshed, and infused with power and vision! It was time to be made whole and complete! What else happens in the King's presence? The Bridegroom of the New Testament returned to escort His bride, the church, into His eternal kingdom! This was THAT time!

As mentioned above, the Oil in the story represents the presence of the Holy Spirit. It is only through hosting the Presence of the Lord that we become carriers or vessels of this powerful Oil. **Through abiding in the Vine and remaining in fellowship with Jesus, we consistently receive a flow of Oil in our lives.** As mentioned in Volume II, "There is no substitute for spending time in the presence of the Lord!" This Oil is the vehicle for the manifestation of God's power in our lives. Isaiah 10:27 reveals the power of this priceless anointing Oil, "It shall come to pass in that day That his burden will be taken away from your shoulder, And his yoke from your neck, **And the yoke shall be destroyed because of the anointing**" (NKJV). Oil was used in biblical times in the anointing ceremony. The Oil is the most valuable thing True Worshippers carry! While the world is **distracted** by gifts, abilities, and achievements, a divine theme of 2020, only the Oil of anointing has the power to break yokes and transform and change lives! Hence, **a shortage of Oil is indicative of broken fellowship and detachment from the Vine.**

The enemy of Purpose uses the things that we haven't dealt with (jealousy, insecurity, fear, unforgiveness, etc.) as fellowship breakers. These works of the flesh, having their origin in our natural nature, are in direct opposition to that which is born of the Spirit (Rom. 8). These issues have the capacity to contaminate, dilute, or pervert our efforts and, more importantly, our ministries and ultimately our purpose. If not buffeted and held in subjection to the power of the Holy Spirit, they become strongholds which manifest themselves in all that we do and result in a diminished Oil supply. Remember, it's the "natural human tendency" stuff that is hostile to the things of the Spirit.

As True Worshippers, we have an obligation to **do the work**! Every single one of us has work! This work is not human ambition or a list of things to keep us busy but our aligning with and submitting to the power and presence of the Holy Spirit, who leads us in our "putting off" what He determines is detrimental or of no kingdom value to us and our "putting on" what we need to fulfill the King's desire. All of the parables in chapter 25 have to do with service and faithfulness. At times, faithfulness is being tested (while the Bridegroom/Master tarries). In Kingdom language, unfaithfulness is the same as wickedness, a shocking revelation when the master scolded the servant who hid his talent in the ground (26).

The young women were buying Oil when the Bridegroom escorted His guests into the wedding feast and locked the door. When they returned, they reiterated a cry heard in chapter 7, beginning with "Lord! Lord!" which ended with the same response from the Lord, **"I don't know you!"** What does this mean? I submit that it is a phrase that points to heart and motivation and indicates that alignment with God's will is missing! These maidens had been busy with various activities and efforts, but they were not supportive of or in keeping with the King's agenda. The Bridegroom responded, "I can assure you I don't even know you." At the end of this parable, we are encouraged to stay awake, aware, keen, and sensitive to the presence and work of God through the Holy Spirit. <u>We are to remain vigilant, faithful, and consistent doing what we know supports our remaining actively intimate with the King.</u> Though we do not know the day or hour of His return, our job is to be ready and prepared whenever He does.

This may be an unpopular idea in our day when truth is relative, but both John 4 and Romans 12 make a distinction between sincere or true worshippers. In these scriptures, we find a vivid portrayal of a Kingdom Demand on a worshipper, who is to live in service to the King, presenting an offering **that God finds acceptable.** This poses an upset to the norm when we consider the obvious but hidden truth, that some offerings are unacceptable. Perhaps our sweet surrender and following the Holy Spirit's lead are the very things that prevent our ever hearing the detrimental and heartbreaking words spoken above, "Depart from Me, I never knew you." **The ultimate sacrifice is quite clear, oneself.** Romans 12:2 (NLT) indicates just how authentic worship and pleasing offerings of service are rendered, by submitting to Him:

> *Don't* **copy the behavior or customs of this world.** *But* **let God transform you** *by* **changing the way you think.** *Then you will* **learn to know God's will for you,** *which is* **good and pleasing and perfect.**

Chapter V

REPRESENTATIVES: ALLEGIANCE & MOTIVATION

I have commissioned them to represent Me just as
You commissioned Me to represent You.
John 17:18 (TPT)

As we align ourselves with the Word, God's Cause becomes our Cause, and the Father Himself becomes our motivation! Receiving Jesus as Lord, we become sons and daughters of God and extensions of the ministry of Jesus Christ, who was the fulfillment of God's will in the earth. As extensions of His ministry, we are carriers of His presence and are His ambassadors or representatives.

A witness is a representative or ambassador who acts or speaks for or in support of another, in this instance, Jesus. Representatives, based on our *chayil* agency, are *chayil* agents who, like Jesus, act on the Father's behalf. They are messengers or promoters of a specific activity, purpose, or cause—in this case, the Cause of Christ. Who better models the lifestyle of a representative given to the advancement of God's Kingdom Agenda than Jesus, fully God and fully man? John 17 (TPT) reveals Jesus's heart as He prayed before He offered Himself up for the redemption of human beings. In His prayer, we hear the heart of God's number 1 representative. If you ever want to know what is of upmost importance to people, listen to them pour their heart out to the Father. What exactly was on Jesus's heart? We were! As Jesus prayed, He demonstrated the attributes of our *chayil* agency, namely a heart of submission, His love for God and those God had given Him, and His relentless commitment to His purpose, even to death. He prayed for His present and future disciples and those who would believe their message.

> *1 Father, the time has come. <u>Unveil the glorious splendor of your Son</u> <u>so that I will magnify Your glory.</u> 2 <u>You have already given Me authority</u> <u>over all people</u> so that <u>I may give eternal life</u> to all those You have given Me. 3 <u>Eternal life means to know and experience You as the only true God</u>, and to <u>know and experience Jesus Christ, as the Son whom You have sent</u>. 4 <u>I have glorified You on earth</u> <u>by faithfully doing everything You've told me to do</u>.*

*5 So my Father, restore me back to the glory that we shared together <u>when we were face-to-face before the universe was created</u>! 6 <u>Father, I have manifested who You really are</u> and <u>I have revealed You to the men and women that You gave to Me</u>. They were Yours, and You gave them to Me, and <u>they have fastened Your Word firmly to their hearts</u>. 7 And now at last <u>they know</u> that <u>everything I have is a gift from YOU</u>, 8 And <u>the very words You gave to Me to speak I have passed on to them</u>. <u>They are convinced</u> that <u>I have come from Your presence</u>, and <u>they have fully believed that You sent me to represent You</u>. 9 So <u>with deep love</u>, <u>I pray for my disciples</u>. I'm not asking on behalf of the unbelieving world, but <u>for those who belong to You, those You have given Me</u>. 10 <u>For all who belong to Me now belong to You. And all who belong to You now belong to Me as well,</u> and **<u>my glory is revealed through their surrendered lives</u>**. (My glory is revealed through their WORSHIP.) 11. Holy Father, I am about to leave this world to return and be with You, but my disciples will remain here. So I ask that by the power of Your name, <u>protect each one that You have given Me, and watch over them so that they will be united as one, even as we are one</u>. 12. While I as with these that You have given Me, <u>I have kept them safe by Your name that You have given Me</u>. Not* *one of them is lost, except the one that was destined to be lost, <u>so that the Scripture would be fulfilled.</u> 13. But now I am returning to You so Father, I pray that <u>they will experience and enter into My joyous delight in You so that it is fulfilled in them and overflows</u>. 14. <u>I have given them Your message</u> and that is why <u>the unbelieving world hates them</u>. **For their allegiance is no longer to this world because I am not of this world**. 15 I am not asking that You remove them from the world, but I <u>ask that You guard their hearts from evil,</u> 16 **For they no longer belong to this world any more than I do**. 17 **Your Word is truth!** So <u>make them holy by the truth</u>. 18 **I have commissioned them to represent Me just as You commissioned Me to represent You**.19 And now <u>I dedicate Myself to them as a holy sacrifice</u> so **that they will live as fully dedicated to God and be made holy by Your truth.** John 17:1-9 (TPT)*

There are so many powerful and revelatory truths in the passage above. Given our working definition of worship, to give oneself over to or to live in a consistent state of surrender to as a slave or servant, we can clearly see that Jesus is a perfect example of such a lifestyle. Jesus showed that our worship extends to the point of representation and ambassadorship. **True Worshippers are ambassadors!**

God is Love (1 John 4), and this entire prayer is laced with the Spirit of Love, care, protection, and provision for those who God had given Jesus, His disciples. Right from the start, Jesus had the Father's honor in mind by asking that His Father unleash His glory, His fullest potential and capacity. This request was not for Jesus to become great, but so that His expression of glory, functioning as God intended, would bring great glory to the Father, Himself! As previously mentioned, this principle rings true for every human being. **When we live out our fullest expression of pre-destined glory, God is greatly honored and glorified!** Next, Jesus clearly stated His purpose, that people might know and experience God as the true God and Jesus as the Son, in an authentic relationship with the Father. God the Father has sent the Son and given Jesus His authority to represent Him. **When you are sent, you are the servant of the One who sent you and have received and carry their authority, power, and message.** The same is true for Christ's disciples, "But you shall receive power after that the Holy Ghost is come upon you, and you shall be witnesses…" (Acts 1:8). Notice that Holy Spirit activation is required to be an effective witness! Jesus then reaffirmed His commitment to the King's agenda, saying that He had glorified the Father, which is to reveal, magnify, or manifest the weight or heaviness of God's magnificence, splendor, brilliance, excellence, power, fullness, and presence. I submit that the way He did this is the exact way that we should—by faithfully doing everything He told Him to do (v4). So, here's the principle again: **when we live in obedient service to the King, which is our worship, we manifest the heaviness or fullness of His presence, and He receives great glory.** Jesus, our finest model of God's representative, said that God had given Him authority, a message, people (who still belonged to God), and had told Him what to do! Jesus glorified God by His worship, and as carriers, true worshippers, and disciples, we are to do the same!

Jesus confirmed His Oneness with the Father as the Word before time began (verse 5) by requesting to be restored back to the glory He had "before the universe was created." Can you imagine Him willfully sacrificing such glory when He took on the form of man for us? Oh, what a love!

Jesus continued, "Father, I've shown them who You really are by providing **Proof of Life** (chapter 7) or the evidence of Your glorious presence contained within Me, the Word, which they have personally embraced." He reaffirmed that the only people He had were the ones the Father had given. As God's representative, Jesus didn't take any credit, stating that those God had given Him knew that everything He had came from the One who had sent Him. **Representatives are sent and arrive to their destination carrying the message of the One who sent them. They understand that it is not their own message that is to be heard; the sole purpose of their arrival is to deliver the message that they carry to its intended recipients.** "They have received Your words and carry them in their hearts. They are convinced that I have come from Your presence" (v. 8). In other words, there is no doubt in their minds *that I am Your representative*. May Jesus's result be ours!

Jesus made it very clear that this prayer was specifically for those the Father had given Him, motivated by His powerful love for His very own disciples or representatives (v. 9). He and the Father together had ownership and were in relationship with those appointed. Verse 10 emphasizes the mission of a True Worshipper: "**...and my glory is revealed through *their surrendered lives*.**" Jesus said, "**...My glory is revealed through their worship,**" not their singing or clapping or joyful dances but via their obedience in doing My will. True Worshippers represent Jesus, and their number-one cause is the Cause of Christ! I cannot reiterate this spiritual truth enough—**to *worship* is to live in a state of continual surrender; it is a life given over to the service of the King as a slave or**

servant to His Cause. Just as Jesus lived to magnify and reveal the presence of the King, we are to do the same. **Through our activated lives of worship and servanthood, we provide Living Proof of the fullness of the presence of the Son of God, expressed through us right here and right now!**

Jesus prayed for our unity, protection, and guidance, and then in verse 13, for divine activation. His request was that the Father would allow His disciples **to experience and enter into His great and exceeding joy**, that Lifeline mentioned above. He asked that it would be fulfilled and overflow in us. Here it is again! We are to be filled to the point of overflow with the presence of the Son, ensuring the sustained supply of Holy Spirit Oil. Jesus made provision for our fulfilling gladness and delightful rejoicing, just as He experienced while living out His Father's desire.

Verse 14 speaks to the disciples' heart, motivation, and allegiance. Jesus said that because He had given the disciples the Father's message and it had been received, they were no longer of this world, just as He wasn't. **Receiving the Son automatically makes one different to their core.** True transformation results in a different value system and worldview, as one's Kingdom Orientation promotes a faith-based Kingdom worldview or perspective. That's the meaning of, "is not of this world." That which drives the average person is not that which drives the Carrier or True Worshipper. I'm reminded of the Scripture which says, "Set your affections on things above, not on things of the earth" (Col. 3:2). **True Worshippers have an affection, cause, and reason that shifted from world-centered to Christ-centered.** Jesus prayed that we would be protected from the evil of this world system (15), a system to which we do not belong. As God guards our hearts, our allegiance will be in the right place. Jesus also asked God to make us holy by His Word, the ultimate Truth. The True Worshipper or representative lives by the Truth, which alone distinguishes them from those whose affections are based in the natural realm. **The Word provides life-vision and guidance for Christ's representatives as it lights or illuminates their paths.**

The true worshipper is taught to love not the world, neither what is in the world (1 John 2:15). This love of the world points to the anti-Christ or anti-God system of the world as outlined in Romans 8:7, where it teaches that the natural man or worldly nature wars against or is hostile to the things of the Spirit. **Not loving the world means not preferring man's system and ways above God's. It's a refusal to live in accordance with or to allow one's life to be rooted or based in the world and a decision to defy the natural tendency to bow, serve, or surrender to (as in worship) the subpar** system which human beings manufacture. It is a resolve to commit to and live by God's righteous Kingdom standards and a reminder that Christ's representatives, *chayil* agents, will only worship (give themselves to) God alone. Here, Jesus confirmed a mandatory shift in allegiance (affection, motivation, and cause). ***This shift automatically occurs from the embrace of and commitment to God's message.*** In the kingdom of God, He alone becomes our cause, our motivation, our reason why. Jesus confirmed that the world hates (opposite of love), is at odds against, and is hostile to the disciple because the disciple represents Him, and the world is hostile to Him. No student is above his teacher (Luke 6:40). A true disciple has **ONE** cause—to advance God's Kingdom agenda by extending the ministry of Jesus Christ. <u>For this carrier, there can be no competition between the Kingdom Demand and the pull of the world.</u> We have been commissioned to represent Jesus (John 17:18).

I recall my graduation from seminary and my oldest son's graduation from the United States Naval Academy. These ceremonies were pretty much the same as all others, except for one unique event—they culminated with a commission. At a certain point within the ceremonies, a commission was received, to serve the cause for which the graduates had been prepared and equipped.

Commission is the same word for sent, *apostello* in the Greek. **It connotes being ordered or sent on a defined mission by a superior, with the focus of the mission always pointing back to the source, the sender (Strong's Greek 649). In this way, the one sent is always connected to the sender.** Now we can see why Jesus always referred to God the Father whenever His validity was questioned. "I'm am not here on My own, for My own. I am here representing He who sent Me." We can also see why servants of YHWH are consistently tempted with selfish ambition and the pride of life, which promotes the aborting of one's mission and separation from the sender. The enemy of Purpose fills the human heart with pride and whispers, "You got this! Do your own thing! You too are great! You don't need God!" He hates what is born of the Spirit, and he acts to deceive us into agreement with him so that he can kill, steal, and destroy IT (John 10:10). If any human could have gotten away with "doing their own thing," it would have been Jesus. Jesus, the only begotten Son, was fully God and fully man. He could have easily aborted the mission, but He didn't. Instead, He consistently referred to "My Father."

Verse 19 confirms Jesus's purpose: **"I offer myself up as an offering so that they will be carriers of my powerful life, and will be able to live with the same devotion to the Father that I have.**

They will become my witnesses, living proof that I live, as they manifest my presence in the earth." Jesus asked the Father to make His disciples holy and set apart for His service by the activation of the power of the Truth in God's Word! We are to be fully dedicated to the King's agenda as affirmed in Matthew 6:33, which teaches us to make the King's agenda and standard of righteousness our very first priority. This is where the True Worshipper's allegiance lies! When we examine Jesus's posture in this prayer, He was **fully submitted to God's will, name, and words, all of which informed His behavior**. This is the biblical standard for Christ's representatives, Carriers, and True Worshippers!

Chapter VI.

KEEPING THE UNITY OF THE SPIRIT: EFFECTIVE WITNESSES

Unity of the Spirit
"…that they may be one as We are one-"

John 17:22 (NIV)

I t's no secret that America's current political persuasions have resulted in great rifts in the Body of Christ. This divide includes racial, social, and cultural tensions that seem irreconcilable. Members of Christ's Body on all sides feel that a great impasse stands in the way of our reality of Christ's love, peace, and unity. True Worshippers, as depicted in John 4, are not to base their truth on what people say or the voices of their day but what Christ the Son says, the ultimate Truth. **The Word of God alone holds the plumb line for living and behavior within the Body of Christ.** Jesus prayed fervently for the unity of His present and future disciples in John 17 (TPT), a prayer which reveals what was important to Him and the concerns of His heart.

*11. Holy Father, I am about to leave this world to return and be with You, but my disciples will remain here. So I ask that by the power of Your name, **protect each one that You have given Me, and watch over them so that they will be united as one, even as we are one**.*

20. And I ask not only for these disciples, but also for all those who will one day believe in Me through their message.

*21. **I pray for them all to be joined together as one even as You and I, Father, are joined together as one. I pray for them to become one with Us so that the world will recognize that You sent Me.***

*22 For the very glory You have given to Me I have given them **so that they will be joined together as one and experience the same unity that we enjoy.***

*23. You live fully in Me and now I live fully in them **so that they will experience perfect unity**, and the world will be convinced that You have sent me, for they will see that **You love each one of them with the same passionate love that You have for Me.***

*24. Father, I ask that You allow everyone that you have given to Me to **be with Me where I am**! Then they will see My full glory- the very splendor You have placed upon Me because You have loved Me even before the beginning of time. 26. I have revealed to them who You are and I will continue to make You even more real to them, **so that they may experience the same endless love that You have for Me, for Your love will now live in them, even as I live in them.***
John 17:11, 20-26 (TPT)

These seven verses point to the unity or oneness of both present and future members of Christ's disciples, which is to be shared and demonstrated. Jesus asked His Father to protect and watch over their unity so that they would be joined together in the same Spirit and manner that He and the Father are (verse 11). He went even further, asking that they not only experience unity but be joined as one and **become One with the Father and Son**. This type of unity within the Body of Christ is to be lived out and witnessed by others. Those who receive His Life demonstrate our One Lord, One Faith, and One Baptism existence, which is a world-wide witness that Jesus is the Messiah, sent by His Father, God (verse 21). To ensure that the very self-same unity that the Father and Son share was also shared by His disciples, **Jesus gave His representatives His own glory,** activating them with the weight or heaviness of His presence, splendor, power, and fullness. <u>This activation was to ignite His characteristics and attributes within His carriers so that the world would see and experience Him through them.</u> Living inside His disciples, Jesus expects His representatives to experience the same perfect unity and love thatz He experiences with His Father. The agape love of Jesus motivates His desire for intimacy, where His disciples can be joined with Him in His presence. Notice that all disciples are included! The Father and Son love every one of their present and future disciples! **Jesus desires each one to be included in His glory, and He intercedes for every single believer all over the world! These believers are of mixed race, creed, and tongue. They are a part of varying cultures, ethnic groups, and social statuses, but they are His!** Jesus took care to seal this Holy Spirit work in us by giving us Himself, declaring that as He lives in us, the love of the Father is alive in us as well! We all have the same spiritual DNA and are all a part of one global and divine family.

We do not necessarily share the same revelations or interpretations, though. Those are our individual God-given glimpses of the Father that He so graciously affords as we pursue Him. It is important to understand that the weight of His glory, splendor, and magnificence CANNOT be confined by, contained within, or limited to our individual, small glimpses of Him. We must accept that God is bigger than our revelations and experiences and is not confined by our opinions, theology, or political persuasions. No! This oneness Christ provides is not contingent on our having common opinions or similar idiosyncrasies but our being united and one in Spirit and Cause as it pertains to the will of God. This unity is a **God-produced harmony between believers, which results from our receiving the Lord and His nature** (Strong's 1775). The love that we receive is Christ's agape love, which is the power that allows us to override natural tendencies in an effort to do what God prefers, that which is beneficial for the entire Body of Christ and the advancement of His Kingdom. As we unanimously serve the Cause of Christ in our concerted surrender, collectively given over as servants in worship to the King, we become Carriers of His forgiveness, freedom, healing, love, and peace and effective witnesses who are able to extend His goodness to others! He is the only One we worship! Let's look at the Kingdom Demand for unity in Ephesians 4 (NIV).

1. As a prisoner for the Lord, then, I urge you to live a life worthy of the calling you have

received. 2. Be completely humble and gentle; be patient, bearing with one another in love.
*3. **Make every effort to keep the unity of the Spirit though the bond of peace**. 4. There is **one body** and **one Spirit**, just as you were called to **one hope** when you were called; 5. **one Lord**, **one faith**, **one baptism**; 6. **one God** and **Father of all**, who is **over all** and **through all** and **in all**. 7.But to each one of us grace has been given as Christ apportioned (divided, allocated, assigned, distributed, shared, dispensed) it.*
Ephesians 4:1-7

Most of us wouldn't hesitate in expressing to others how much we love God and are devoted to Him! In fact, our corporate gatherings are filled with such expressions. We take our callings seriously, but are we serious enough to be united or joined with those who look nothing like us, speak a different language, or voted for the other candidate? In the passage above, we hear a divine call to rise to the Kingdom Standard of love. The plumb line is one of gentleness, patience, love, and peace. The Kingdom Demand is to do all that is in your power to keep the unity of the Spirit through the bond of peace. **In other words, as carriers and true worshippers, the Cause of Christ unites us**. Nothing else matters where the Kingdom of God is concerned. When we represent Him, speak His words, and deliver His message, we unite in Kingdom advancement! All of the other personal preferences, interpretations, glimpses, etc. do not matter. They are personal! Remember—the witness understands that only the message of the sender needs to be heard.

How many churches are there? How many Bodies of Christ are there? How many Lords are there? The resounding answer to all of these is **ONE**! Regardless of the great divides, gulfs, riffs, disagreements, bitterness, misunderstandings, error, and mistakes, all followers of Christ have the same faith, Lord, hope, and baptism. There is **ONE God and Father**, over, through, and in **all,** regardless of skin tone, dialect, country, neighborhood, or political persuasion. No human being has the power to change this! Further, the Word says that every single believer has been assigned an allocation of God's grace or glory to express on His behalf (verse 7) so that He will receive glory! That allocation of grace is our calling, our life-assignment, our part, our purpose, our glimpse. Romans 12:2 (NLT) confirms, "In His grace, God has given us different gifts for doing certain things well…" These gifts align with the grace we carry. No individual glimpse is the entire measure of God's fullness, glory, or grace. **When we consider our glimpse and expression of His glory as the entire measure of Christ, we err!** In 1 Corinthians 13:9 (NLT), it says it this way, "Now our knowledge is partial and incomplete, and even the gift of prophecy reveals only part of the whole picture!"

The many-membered Body flows out of the wisdom of God. God has designed it so that each one is loved, valuable, and necessary. 1 Corinthians 12 (NIV) confirms that each part of the Body is baptized by and filled with one Holy Spirit. Regardless of natural and human differences, there is to be no division within the Body.

> *12. Just as a body, though one, has many parts, but all its many parts form one body, so it is with Christ.*
> *13. For we were all baptized by one Spirit so as to form one body-whether Jews or Gentiles, slave or free-and we were all given the one Spirit to drink.*
> *14. Even so the body is not made up of one part but many…*
> *24 …But God has put the body together, giving greater honor to the parts that lacked it,*
> *25. so that there should be no division in the body, but that its parts should have equal concern for each other.*
> *1 Corinthians 12:12-14, 24-25 (NIV)*

John 13:34-35 declares a Kingdom Demand in the form of a commandment for Jesus's disciples to demonstrate the same agape love for each other as He had done. Verse 35 confirms that demonstrating agape love for one another is an indicator of Christ's true followers or True Worshippers:

34. "So I give you now a new commandment: Love each other just as much as I have loved you.
35. For when you demonstrate the same love I have for you by loving one another, everyone will know that you're my true followers."

Colossians 3 (MSG) provides unity tools or fruit of the Spirit, which makes cultivating the peace of Christ in this new life of agape love a reality:

*12-14 So, ch**osen by God for this new life of (agape) love**, dress in the wardrobe God picked out for you: compassion, kindness, humility, quiet strength, discipline. Be even-tempered, content with second place, quick to forgive an offense. Forgive as quickly and completely as the Master forgave you. And regardless of what else you put on, **wear love**. It's your basic, all-purpose garment. Never be without it.*
***15-17** Let the peace of Christ keep you in tune with each other, in step with each other. None of this going off and doing your own thing. And cultivate thankfulness. Let the Word of Christ—the Message—have the run of the house. Give it plenty of room in your lives.*
Colossians 3:12-17 (MSG)

Chapter VII

PROOF OF LIFE

Living in Response to the Holy Spirit as Modern-Day Deliverers

*17. This is what I will do in the last days-**I will pour out my Spirit on everybody** and cause your sons and daughters to prophesy, and your young men will see visions, and your old men will experience dreams from God. 18. **The Holy Spirit will come upon all my servants, men and women alike**, and they will prophesy. 19. I will reveal startling signs and wonders in the sky above and mighty miracles on the earth below.*
Acts 2:17-19 (TPT)

As the world continues to fight the COVID-19 virus and its variants with vaccine distribution efforts, one of the beautiful lessons of 2020 is that God is a God of the nations, and He is a God of the people. Long gone are the days when Holy Spirit activation and demonstration was reserved for those identified as clergy, five-fold, and other spiritual leaders. In Acts 2:17-19, Peter recited Joel 2:28, when the prophet foretold of a powerful time when the Spirit of God would be poured out on all servants! It's an activation that includes every member of Christ's Body!

This kingdom activation is the reason why the shift in our perception of worship is so important. If we continue to consider worship as simply the time between 10:00 am and 12:00 pm on Sundays and once or twice during the week, at the start of our corporate gatherings, we will remain as spectators and forfeit our rights to be participants in His Kingdom! Why? **The former perspective of worship is a "form of godliness" or worship, which denies the power thereof, only serving to soothe our brokenness instead of healing it, giving us warm feelings which temporarily lift us above the negativity we entertain instead of setting us free from it with the free-indeed power of the Son.** The lift is temporary because it's contingent on the music, the place, and the people; learn the lesson of the "Great Pandemic." The sweet surrender of worship is about power-filled lives motivated by the presence of God, bearing fruit that remain. It's about the living that happens when we leave the corporate gatherings and demonstrate *Proof of Life*!

Proof of Life is a phrase conventionally used in kidnappings, when evidence is requested which indicates that the one taken is still alive. When presenting Proof of Life, **unmistakable evidence is presented** which proves that the victim has life. **The significance of Proof of Life is that it is convincing and encourages participation. Proof of Life confirms Life**, and as Christ's ambassadors or representatives, we are to be witnesses and bear living proof as carriers of His Life and Power, manifested in the earth through His activated chayil agents.

Proof of Life in the lives of God's children is His divine power! "But you will receive power [*chayil (Hebrew) or dounamis (Greek)*] *when the* Holy Ghost comes upon you. And you will be my witnesses, telling people about Me everywhere- in Jerusalem, throughout Judea, in Samaria, and to the ends of the earth" (Acts 1:8 NLT). **We must remember that we do not become effective witnesses without the divine activation of the Holy Spirit.** We cannot adequately represent Christ without His power! This power, which transforms lives and produces fruit, is only gained through intimacy with the Lord, the King, the Holy Spirit. The narrative of the lame man dramatically holds his complete transformation by activated Carriers of the Lord's presence and power in tension against temple-goers whose natural efforts only temporarily helped the cripple man, leaving him in the same state for many years (Acts 3 NLT).

1. Peter and John went to the Temple one afternoon to take part in the three o'clock prayer service. 2. As they approached the Temple, a man lame from birth was being carried in. Each day **he was put beside the Temple gate***, the one called the Beautiful Gate,* **so he could beg from the people going into the Temple***. 3. When he saw Peter and John about to enter, he asked them for some money. 4. Peter and John looked at him intently, and Peter said,* **"Look at us!"** *5. The lame man looked at them eagerly, expecting some money. 6. But Peter said,* **"I don't have any silver or gold for you. But I'll give you what I have. In the name of Jesus Christ the Nazarene, get up and walk!"** *7. Then Peter took the lame man by the right hand and helped him up. And as he did,* **the man's feet and ankles were instantly healed and strengthened.** *8. He jumped up, stood on his feet, and began to walk! Then, walking, leaping, and praising God, he went into the Temple with them. 9. All the people*

*saw him walking and heard him praising God.
10 When they realized he was
the lame beggar they had seen so often at the
Beautiful Gate, they were absolutely
astounded! 11. They all rushed out in amaze-
ment to Solomon's Colonnade, where the
man was holding tightly to Peter and John.
Acts 3:1-11 (NLT)*

This narrative opens with a man who was born lame sitting at the Temple by the Beautiful Gate, which was believed to receive the most traffic. This man had spent decades of his entire life begging alms as people passed him on their way into the Temple. You might ask, "How did he get to the gate?" Well, there were those, touched with human compassion, who would faithfully place him at this entrance so that his begging would be heard by as many attendants as possible. On one particular day, he laid eyes on two men, representatives of Jesus Christ and Carriers of His presence and power! These were not just temple-goers; they were True Worshippers! **It's safe to say that the day he laid eyes on them was the day his life changed!** When Peter and John approached the Beautiful Gate, the beggar did what he had always done; however, this time, he encountered Kingdom Ambassadors who carried the authority and power of the One who commissioned them!

He didn't know that on this particular day there was an **Emergence of True Worshippers!**

Peter's response to the beggar, **"I don't have money for you today, but I will give you what I have,"** says it all! I imagine Peter saying, "Sir, you receive money every week, and it hasn't relieved you! You are still begging! Earthly things have left you dry. **What I have is the power of the Holy Ghost that will transform your life forever!** I am a Carrier of the power and presence of the Son! Guess what, sir? After this encounter with the presence of YHWH, you will never need to be carried here to beg again! You will walk into the temple with everyone else! Your life will change forever! Now, in the name of Jesus, rise up and walk!"

The people's solution for this lame man's problem involved his needing their help every single week to receive the same subpar result. He was not only lame physically but spiritually and emotionally for he was totally dependent on others for his needs! True Worshippers, as those who seek **first** the King's Kingdom and His righteousness, **defy the natural, human tendency to make and keep themselves as the central focal point of people, places, and events.** Not to do so would be an oxymoron, as the true meaning of worship is to give oneself over to another as a slave or servant. This battle is lifelong, as our flesh is never redeemed. This is why the Scriptures say, "I buffet my body…" (1 Cor. 9:27), and again, "He must increase and I must decrease" (John 3:30). The temptation to draw attention to self is powerful yet subtle, often disguising itself as humility or service. Partnering and aligning with the Holy Spirit, who leads into all Truth, is never out of style and always necessary. The Truth of the Word of God is quick and powerful, able to discern thoughts and motives, and when it does, we bring every thought into obedience to Christ. This is necessary and mandatory because even the strongest, most disciplined Christian can fall prey to a spirit of selfish ambition and the works of the flesh. This man did not need a gimmick; he needed the Giver of miracles! As stated above, representatives of Christ on a mission, deliver **only** what they carry from the One who sent them.

This story contrasts the difference between human ability and God's power through the human and depicts how ineffective we are as witnesses, living proof of God's powerful presence, without consistent divine encounters and activation. It also shows how miserable others are when we tolerate life without intimacy with our Heavenly Father, and, as a result, without the power included in our divine inheritance. Here, God through man was elevated, as we study the lives of those who willingly glorified Him by allowing His power through them to bless His creation! What Peter carried did not originate with him; it was supernatural, other-worldly, and far superior to what any human could ever imagine or achieve. This narrative is a fine example of what it means to live in response to the Holy Spirit. May we surrender to God so that His desire can be revealed through us!

Volume 2 of this series contains a powerful teaching regarding knowing the Shepherd's voice! Suffice it to say that Holy Spirit training and discipline are required to cultivate sensitivity to the Spirit and presence of God, and the Scriptures bear witness that when God places a divine deposit on the inside of someone, at some point, He will place a demand on that which belongs to Him. Living in the Light of His presence facilitates the development and maturity of that deposit! God will activate that deposit with His power at the right time so that it will transform the lives of others. **Activation is not a list of activities, good deeds, or busyness but is specific to the will and desire of God, His unique purpose in blessing and delivering His creation.** Activation results in bearing much fruit and bringing the Father great glory. That's right! True Worshippers are Carriers of Christ's Light and Life which destroy Satan's dark deeds. Luke said it this way:

Now you understand that I have imparted to you my authority to trample over his kingdom. You will trample upon every demon before you and overcome every power Satan possesses. Absolutely nothing will harm you as you walk in this authority. Luke 10:19 (TPT)

Appearing to His disciples after His resurrection, Jesus pronounced divine peace upon them, a peace that is beyond understanding, for those who would represent Him. He equipped them by activating His power, the Holy Spirit, in their lives and affirmed their assignment and participation as His ambassadors. He clearly defined the cause—to preach the forgiveness of sins and to share the Gospel of the Kingdom.

*21. Jesus repeated his greeting, "Peace to you! And he told them, Just as the Father has sent me, I'm now sending you. 22 Then, taking a deep breath, he blew on them and said, **Receive the Holy Spirit.** 23. I send you to preach the forgiveness of sin-and people's sins will be forgiven. But if you don't proclaim the forgiveness of their sins, they will remain guilty. John20:21-23 (TPT)*

The intercession of Jesus for us in John 17 fills us with great hope! If ever a prayer is to be answered, it's the one the Son prays to the Father! The beauty of representing Christ as Carriers and True Worshippers is that He gives us all that we need to fulfill His desire to answer the Holy Spirit's call! He then places a Kingdom Demand on that which belongs to Him. Above, Joel spoke of God's sons and daughters being saturated with His presence to present **Proof of Life** in the last days, and Jesus confirmed a similar activation for service by blowing the breath of Life and commanding the disciples to receive the Holy Spirit!

CLOSING PRAYER

May we immerse ourselves in the outpouring of the presence of God. May we become activated Carriers of all that we have divinely received and worship Him in a manner He finds acceptable by giving ourselves over to Him and living a life of sweet surrender and servanthood. May we embrace our ambassadorship and represent Him well. May we give way to the promptings of the Holy Spirit and Emerge as True Worshippers who give their allegiance to Him and receive their motivation from Him. May we defy the urge to abort the mission, giving people ourselves instead of the divine deposit that we carry. May we embrace *the such as I have* Kingdom lifestyle and bring great glory to God just as Peter did by healing and delivering the lame man…

> *12. With the crowd surrounding him, Peter said to them all, "People of Israel, listen to me! Why are you so amazed by this healing? Why do you stare at us? We didn't make this crippled man walk by our own power or authority. 13. The God of our ancestors, the God of Abraham, Issac,*

and Jacob has done this...15. You have killed the Prince of Life! But God raised Him from the dead, and we stand here as witnesses to the fact."
Acts 3:12-15 (TPT)

CPSIA information can be obtained
at www.ICGtesting.com
Printed in the USA
BVHW092252111121
621213BV00011B/1142